1 Foreword

This Exam Preparation book is intended for those preparing for the ITIL® V3 Intermediate Lifecycle Stream: Service Transition Exam.

The Art of Service is an Accredited Training Organization for this program and has been training this course for more than 8 years. The strategies and content in this book is a result of experience and understanding of the ITIL® Service Transition Program, and the exam requirements.

This book is **not** a replacement for completing the course. This is a study aid to assist those who have completed an accredited course and preparing for the exam.

Do not underestimate the value of your own notes and study aids. The more you have, the more prepared you will be.

While it is not possible to pre-empt every question and content that MAY be asked in the Intermediate Service Transition exam, This Book covers the main concepts covered within the ITIL Intermediate Service Transition Syllabus and a Practice Exam (created by The Art of Service).

Each Process contains a summarized overview of key knowledge. These overviews are designed to help you to reference the knowledge gained through the course.

Due to licensing rights, we are unable to provide actual APMG Exams. However, the study notes and sample exam questions in this book will allow you to more easily prepare for an APMG ITIL® Service Transition exam.

Ivanka Menken
Executive Director
The Art of Service

ITIL® is a Registered Community Trade Mark of OGC (Office of Government Commerce, London, UK), and is Registered in the U.S. Patent and Trademark Office.

2 Table of Contents

1. Foreword 1
2. Table of Contents 2
3. ITIL® v3 Certification Pathway 4
4. Exam Specifics 5
5. Exam Prerequisites 6
6. Exam Hints 7
7. The Art of Service Objective Tree 9
8. Study Notes 10
9. IT Service Management 11
10. ITIL ® v3 Service Lifecycle 14
11. Service Transition 15
12. Change Management 17
13. Release and Deployment 22
14. Service Validation and Testing 27
15. Evaluation 32
16. Service Asset and Configuration Management 35
17. Knowledge Management 39
18. Service Transition - Technology and Implementation 41
19. Service Transition Roles 45
20. Practice Exam 46
21. Answer Guide 90
22. ACRONYMS 99
23. Glossary 101
24. References 104

Notice of Rights
All rights reserved. No part of this book may be reproduced or transmitted in any form by any means, electronic, mechanical, photocopying, recording, or otherwise, without the prior written permission of the publisher.

Notice of Liability
The information in this book is distributed on an "As Is" basis without warranty. While every precaution has been taken in the preparation of the book, neither the author nor the publisher shall have any liability to any person or entity with respect to any loss or damage caused or alleged to be caused directly or indirectly by the instructions contained in this book or by the products described in it.

Trademarks
Many of the designations used by manufacturers and sellers to distinguish their products are claimed as trademarks. Where those designations appear in this book, and the publisher was aware of a trademark claim, the designations appear as requested by the owner of the trademark. All other product names and services identified throughout this book are used in editorial fashion only and for the benefit of such companies with no intention of infringement of the trademark. No such use, or the use of any trade name, is intended to convey endorsement or other affiliation with this book.

3 ITIL® v3 Certification Pathway

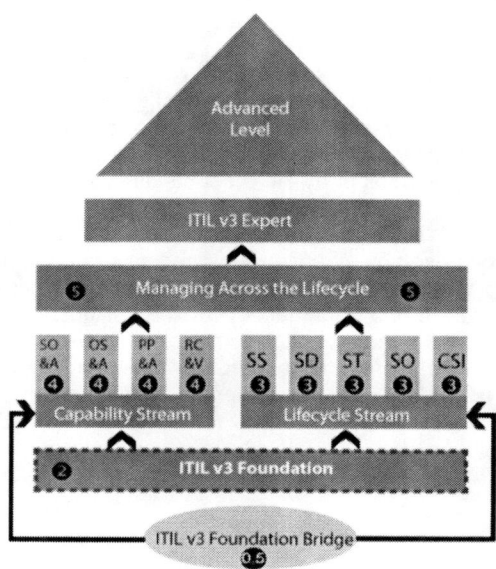

Since the launch of ITIL v3 in July 2007, a new certification path was also released. This new path encompasses all the new v3 Programs, ending in the possible attainment of "Expert Status". The figure below demonstrates the possible pathways that you could take to achieve the Expert status.

To achieve Expert status, you are required to gain a minimum of 22 points by completing various ITIL® v3 programs:
- You must complete the v3 Foundation Program (2 points)
- You must complete the Managing Across the Lifecycle Program (5 points)
- The remaining 15 points must come from The Intermediate Stream (Capability and Lifecycle Programs)

(The numbers on each program indicate the point's value.)

It is yet to be finalized how the "Advanced Level" can be achieved, but is expected to be based on demonstration of practical experience in ITIL and IT Service Management.

4 Exam Specifics

The APMG ITIL® v3 Intermediate Service Transition exam is:
- Multiple choice exam
- 90 minutes in length
- 8 scenario based questions
- Pass mark is 70%
- Closed book exam
- Scaled Marking system:
  - Most correct answer – 5 marks
  - Next – 3 marks
  - Next – 1 mark
  - 1 answer – 0 marks.

It is possible to do a paper based or a web based exam. (Please check with your Accredited Examination Centre for more information on this).

5 Exam Prerequisites

In order to sit the ITIL Intermediate Service Transition Exam, you MUST have an ITIL v3 Foundation Certificate or ITIL v2 Foundation plus Bridge Certificate and completion of an accredited program from an ITIL Accredited Training Provider.

6 Exam Hints

When it comes time to sit your exam, you need to do this through an accredited Authorized Examination Center. You may have the option to do the exam as web or paper based. Either way, you will be given a paper copy of the Scenarios. A good thing!

(Especially of you are doing web based – do not waste time opening web versions of the scenario – use the paper ones).

Do not be fooled by the "only 8 questions" concept. These questions are designed to test you - not only your knowledge, but also your understanding and application of the theory. You have 90 minutes, which means roughly 11 minutes per question. Most questions come with their own case study/scenario. You need to CAREFULLY read the scenario, then the question, then the scenario again.

There are 4 possible answers – 1 is totally WRONG! And usually it is obvious to see which that is. If we do our math – you need 28/40 to pass. This means that if the answers are based on a 5/3/1/0 scale – you really cannot afford to get any 0 answers. You MUST get at least 2 x 5 mark answers and the remaining averaging 3's (to get minimum of 28) …. So you DO need to know your stuff.

THINK Business! – Remember – as "Techies", we tend to get caught up in "our" IT world. The ITIL v3 lifecycle and in particular ITSM is customer centric… THINK THIS WAY when answering questions!

Know your content – know your order. This study guide gives you a solid revision approach to this course – but does not cover ALL content (that's why you do the course). Make sure you know what makes up a policy/plan/ and the activities for each process, as well as who does what.

Case study hints

- Identify main process/concept being tested
- Identify the "issue/problem" faced within the scenario – there will always be one – your role is to resolve that issue.
- Once you have read the associated question, go back and identify/confirm that you are on the right track

Question hints

- The 4 possible answers will appear to be similar – you need to read the possible answers carefully.
- Eliminate the most obvious "wrong answer"... Things to look for:
    - Order of activities
    - Red herring activities
    - Wrong processes
    - Wrong description
- From the remaining 3 responses – start to identify similarities/differences – this will help you to eliminate the next response generally – the differences will be a hint that one of them is incorrect – you have to decide which one
- It is probable that the "most correct" response would have the correct order of activities/ descriptions and "just that little bit more".
- DO NOT assume that the longest response is the most correct one
- Expect a "phase" question – while most questions are obvious what it is testing (i.e. process) – you could expect to get a "big picture" question asking about Service Transition in general – so make sure you understand your related phases.

7   The Art of Service Objective Tree

This Objective Tree is a very useful tool for understanding and "tunneling" down into how ITSM can contribute to achieving a corporate objective. This helps us to better understand how the Service Lifecycle can contribute to achieving the Business objectives

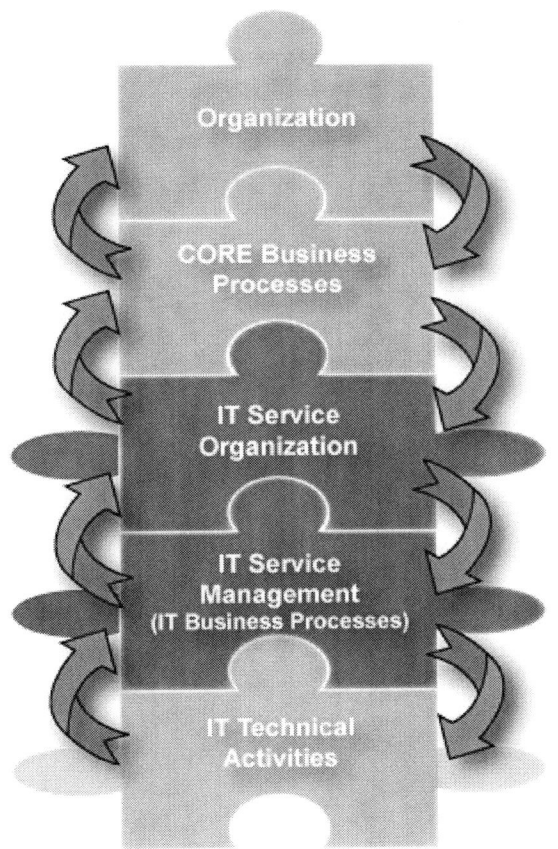

The aim of the Objective tree is to walk down the tree to understand **HOW** each level of the organization is assisted in achieving their objective by receiving support from the level below.

Once you get to the bottom, you then walk back up the tree, giving example of **WHY** each would be of benefit to the one above in achieving its objectives.

ITIL contributes in the darker IT aspects in providing quality IT Service Management.

8 Study Notes

The following Study notes are broken down into the following topics:
- o   Service Management as a concept and relevant terminology
- o   ITIL Service Lifecycle as a concept and relevant terminology
- o   Service Transition Phase and processes
- o   Implementing Service Transition

Again these study notes are not intended to replace an accredited ITIL Service Transition Program. These notes are supplementary and may not include EVERY concept that may be tested.

9 IT Service Management

9.1 Basic Concepts:

9.1.1 ITSM is the effective and efficient process driven management of quality IT Services. The added value to ITSM is that is business aligned and maintains a holistic Service Lifecycle approach.

9.1.2 Four Perspectives of ITSM (as found in Service Design Phase):
- People
- Partners
- Process
- Products

9.1.3 **Why Service Management?**
- Business more **dependent** on IT
- **Complexity** of technology increases
- Customers **demand** more
- Environment becomes more **competitive**
- Focus on controlling **costs** of IT
- Low customer **satisfaction**
- Falling **credibility** of some IT organizations

9.1.4 **Roles**: There are many roles associated with ITIL processes. Each process should have a Process Manager e.g. Incident Manager. It is also reasonable for each Phase to have a Manager, e.g. Service Design Manager.

9.2 Key Terms:

Process: a set of coordinated activities combining and implementing resources and capabilities in order to produce an outcome and *provide value to customers or stakeholders*.

Service: a means of delivering value to customers by facilitating outcomes customers want to achieve without the ownership of specific costs or risks.

IT Infrastructure: all the hardware, software, networks, facilities, services and support elements that are required to *develop, test, deliver, monitor, control* and *support* IT Services

ITSM: A set of specialized organizational capabilities for providing value to customers in the form of services.

Capabilities: The functions and processes utilized to manage services. Capabilities are intangible assets of an organization and cannot be purchased, but must be developed and matured over time.

Resources: A generic term that includes IT Infrastructure, people, money or anything else that might help to deliver an IT service. Resources are also considered to be tangible assets of an organization.

Good Practice: (also referred to as Best Practice) That which is successful in "**wide industry use**"

Functions: A team or group of *people* and the tools they use to carry out one or more Processes or Activities. Functions provide units of organization responsible for specific outcomes.

Customer: refers to the person who "pays" for the service, or has the authority to request a service.

User: An organization's staff member/employee who "uses" the IT service

System: refers to a range of repositories for storing and accessing information – can include databases, Filing cabinets, storage cupboards etc

10 ITIL ® v3 Service Lifecycle

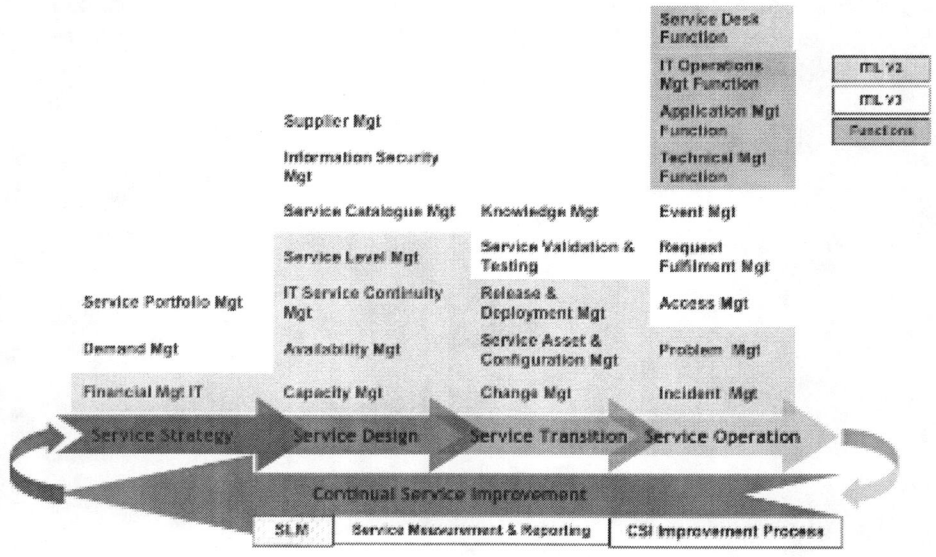

Version 3 maintains a holistic view covering the entire lifecycle of a service, no longer does ITIL just answer the how questions, but also **why?**

•Why does a customer need this service?
•Why should the customer purchase services from us?
•Why should we provide (x) levels of availability, capacity and continuity?

By first asking these questions it enables a service provider to provide overall **strategic objectives** for the IT organization, which will then be used to direct *how* services are **designed, transitioned, supported and improved** in order to deliver maximum value to customers and stakeholders.

11 Service Transition

Service Transition Processes:

- Change Management
- Release And Deployment
- Transition, Planning and Support
- Service Validation and Testing
- Service Evaluation
- Service Asset and Configuration Management
- Knowledge Management

Objective:

- Plan and manage the resources to establish successfully a new or changed service into production within the predicted cost, quality and time estimates.
- Ensure there is a minimal unpredicted impact on the production environment, services, operations and support organization.
- Increase the customer, user and Service Management staff satisfaction with the Service Transition practices including deployment of the new or changed service, communications, release documentation, training and knowledge transfer.
- Increase proper use of the services and underlying applications and technology solutions.
- Provide clear and comprehensive plans that enable the customer and business change projects to align their activities with the Service Transition plans

Basic Concepts:

11.1.1 Two types of significant Service Management processes found within the Service Transition phase.

1. Processes that support the entire service lifecycle
- Change Management
- Service Asset & Configuration Management
- Knowledge Management

2. Processes within Service Transition
- Transition Planning & Support
- Release & Deployment Management
- Service Testing & Validation
- Evaluation

11.1.2 Value of Service Transition:

- Effective Service Transition can significantly improve a Service provider's ability to handle high volumes of change and releases across its Customer base.
- Ability to act quickly and stay ahead of the curve
- The success rate of changes and releases
- Transition Management of mergers, acquisition and transfers etc
- Predictions of service levels and warranties
- Timely cancellation or changes to maintenance contracts
- Risk understanding
- Competitive edge

11.1.3 Creating Service Value:

Utility + Warranty = Value
- Utility (fit for purpose) features and support of service
- Warranty (fit for use) – defines levels of availability, capacity, security, continuity

12 Change Management

Objective: The objective of this process is to ensure that changes are recorded and then evaluated, authorized, prioritized, planned, tested, implemented, documented and reviewed in a controlled manner

12.1 Basic Concepts:

12.1.1 Change Management – Value

- Prioritizing and responding to change proposals
- Implementing the agreed changes
- Contribute to requirements
- Reduce failed changes
- Meeting agreed timescales
- Tracking changes
- Making informed estimations
- Assessing risk
- Reducing Mean Time To Restore Services metrics
- Liaise with business for managing changes

12.1.2 Change Management Policies

- Creating a culture of Change Management – with zero tolerance on unauthorized changes.
- Aligning the service Change Management process with business, project and stakeholder Change Management
- Prioritization of changes
- Establishing accountability and responsibilities
- Segregation of duty controls
- Establish a single focal point for changes
- Prevent people who are not authorized to make changes from accessing production environment
- Integration with other Service Management processes
- Change windows

- Performance and risk evaluation
- Performance measures for the process

12.1.3 Requirements and consideration for design of the Change Management process include:

- Requirements of the business, IT organization and other stakeholders involved
- Approach to eliminating unauthorized changes
- Identification and classification
- Organization, roles and responsibilities
- Stakeholders
- Grouping and relating changes
- Procedures
- Interfaces

12.1.4 Change Model Process should include:

- Steps to take to handle the change including handling issues and unexpected events.
- Chronological order the steps should be taken in
- Responsibilities
- Timescales and thresholds for completion of actions
- Escalation procedures.

Models are usually input in to the Change Management support tools in use and the tools then automate the handling, management, reporting and escalation of the process.

12.1.5 Overall Change Management activities include:

- Planning and controlling changes
- Change and release scheduling
- Communications
- Change decision making and change authorization
- Ensuring there are remediation plans
- Measurement and control

- Management reporting
- Understanding the impact of change
- Continual improvement.

12.1.6 7 R's of Change Management

1. Who RAISED the change?
2. What is the REASON for the change?
3. What is the RETURN required from the change?
4. What are the RISKS involved in the change?
5. What RESOURCES are required to deliver the change?
6. Who is RESPONSIBLE for the build, test and implementation of the change?
7. What is the RELATIONSHIP between this change and other changes?

12.1.7 Inputs:

- Policy and strategies for change and release
- RFC
- Change Proposal
- Plans e.g. change, transition, release, deployment, test, evaluation and remediation.
- Current change schedule
- Current assets or configuration items
- Test results, test reports and evaluation report

12.1.8 Outputs:

- Rejected RFC's
- Approved RFC's
- Change to the services
- New, changed or disposed assets and CI's
- Change schedule
- Authorized change plans
- Change documents and records.

12.1.9 Interface with Service Operation Activities
- Raising RFC's
- Participation in CAB or CAB/EC
- Implementing changes
- Back out changes
- Defining and maintaining change models
- Receiving change schedules
- Standard changes

12.1.10 Challenges

- Change in culture
- Bypassing
- Optimal link with Configuration Management
- Commitment of the supplier(s) to the process
- Commitment of the management

12.1.11 Metrics

- # of changes implemented which met customer agreed requirements
- Benefits of change
- Reduction in # of disruption to services
- Reduction in # of unauthorized changes
- Reduction in backlog of RFC's
- Reduction in # and % of unplanned changes and emergency fixes
- Change success rate
- Reduction in # of failed changes
- Incidents attributable to changes
- % accuracy in change estimations

12.2 Key Terms:

RFC: Request for Change:
Standard form to capture and process ALL Changes to any CI

Change Schedule:
Schedule of Approved Changes and the planned implementation dates.

PSO = Projected Service Outage:
A document that identifies the effect of planned changes, maintenance activities and test plans on agreed service levels.

CAB = Change Advisory Board:
Provide expert advice to Change Management, with representatives from Financial, IT background and customers

ECAB = Emergency CAB: Subgroup of CAB with authority to make urgent change decisions.

PIR: Post Implementation Review

13 Release and Deployment

Objectives:
- There are clear and comprehensive release and deployment plans
- A release package can be built, installed, tested and deployed efficiently
- A new or changed service and its enabling systems, technology and organization are capable of delivering the agreed service requirements
- There is minimal unpredicted impact on the production services, operations and support organization
- Customer, users and Service Management staff are satisfied with the Service Transition practices and outputs.

13.1 Basic Concepts:

Release and Deployment – Value:

- Delivering change, faster, at optimum cost and minimized risk
- Assuring customers and users can use the new or changed service in a way that supports the business goals
- Improving consistency in implementation approach across the business, change, service teams, suppliers and customers
- Contributing to meeting auditable requirements for traceability through Service Transition.

13.1.1 Release and Deployment plans:

- Scope and content of release
- Risk assessment and risk profile for the release
- Organizations and stakeholders affected by the release
- Stakeholders that approved the change request for the release and/or deployment team responsible for the release
- Approach to working with stakeholders and deployment groups to determine the: delivery and deployment strategy,

resources for the release and deployment and amount of change that can be absorbed.

13.1.2 Build and test planning:

- Developing test plans from the service design package
- Establishing logistics, lead times and build times
- Testing the build and related procedures
- Scheduling the build and test activities
- Assigning resources, roles and responsibilities to perform key activities
- Security procedures and checks
- Technical support
- Preparing build and test environments
- Managing test databases and test data
- Software asset and license management
- Configuration Management – configuration audit, build and baseline management.
- Defining and agreeing the build exit and entry criteria

13.1.3 Types of Releases:

- Big Bang vs. Phased
- Push vs. Pull
- Manual vs. Automatic

13.1.4 Release and Deployment Models define:

- Release structure
- Exit and entry criteria
- Controlled environments
- Roles and responsibilities
- Release promotion and configuration baseline model
- Template release and deployment schedules
- Supporting systems, tools and procedures
- Handover activities and responsibilities

13.1.5 Inputs:

- Authorized RFC
- Service Package, SLP
- SDP
- IT Service & Business Continuity Plans
- Technology and procurement standards
- Acquired service assets and components
- Build models and plans
- Environment requirements and specifications
- Release policy and release design
- Release and deployment models
- Exit and entry criteria for each stage.

13.1.6 Outputs:

- Release and deployment plan
- Completed RFC's
- Service notification
- Updated Service Catalogue
- New tested service capability and environment including SLA's etc
- New or changed Service Management documentation
- Service Package, SLP
- SLA, OLA, UC
- Service model
- New or changed service reports
- Tested continuity plans
- Complete and accurate configuration item list
- Service Capacity plan
- Service Transition report.

13.1.7 Challenges

- Developing standard performance measures and measurement methods across projects and suppliers
- Dealing with projects and suppliers where estimated delivery dates are inaccurate and there are delays in scheduling Service Transition activities
- Understanding the different stakeholder perspectives that underpin effective risk management for the change impact assessment and test activities
- Building a thorough understanding of risks that have impacted or may impact successful Service Transition of services and releases
- Encouraging a risk management culture where people share information and take a pragmatic and measured approach to risk.

13.1.8 Metrics:

Customers or business:

- Variance from service performance required by customers
- # of incidents against the service (low and reducing)
- Increased customer and user satisfaction with the services delivered
- Decreased customer dissatisfaction.

Service Providers:

- Reduced resources/cost to diagnose and fix incidents/problems in deployment and production
- Increased adoption of the Service Transition common framework of standards and re-useable processes
- Reduced discrepancies in configuration audits compared with the real world.

13.2 Key Terms:

Release: A collection of **authorized** Changes to an IT Service. Also known as a Release Package

Release Unit: A Release Unit describes the portion of a service of IT infrastructure that is normally released together according to the organizations release policy. The unit may vary depending on type(s) or item(s) of service asset or service component such as hardware or software.

Definitive Media Library (DML): The secure library in which the definitive authorized versions of all media CIs are stored and protected. The DML should include definitive copies of purchased software (along with license documents or information) as well as software developed on site.

Definitive Spares: Physical storage of all *spare IT components and assemblies maintained at the same level as those within the live environment*. These can then be used when needed for additional systems or in the recovery from Incidents.

Details recorded in the CMDB, controlled by Release Management.

Early Life Support: engaging the Development teams in the "early life" of a newly transitioned service to assist with initial support, incident management and rapid knowledge development.

14 Service Validation and Testing

Objectives:
- Provide confidence
- Validate that a service is 'fit for purpose'
- Assure a service is 'fit for use'
- Confirm that a new customer and stakeholder requirements for the new or changed service are correctly defined

14.1 Basic Concepts:

14.1.1 Service Validation and Testing - Business Value:

- The key value to the business and customers from Service Validation and Testing is in terms of the established degree of confidence that a new or changed service will deliver the value and outcomes required of it, and understanding the risks.
- The required degree of confidence varies depending on the customer's business requirements and pressures of an organization.

14.1.2 Service Validation and Testing - Policies:

- Service Quality Policy
- Risk Policy
- Service Transition Policy
- Release Policy
- Change Management Policy.

14.1.3 Service V Model

- ***The Service V Model*** is used to provide a framework for organizing the levels of testing and validation required for new or changed services in order to ***justify release to the customer for trial and assessment.***
- The **left hand side** represents the specification of the service acceptance/review criteria, from high-level functional requirements down to the detailed release and component criteria. Primarily developed in **Service Design Phase.**
- The **right hand side** focuses on the validation and test activities that are performed against the specifications defined on the left hand side, with direct involvement by the equivalent party on the right hand side (**Service Transition Phase**).
- It shows that validation and test planning should begin early in the life of a Service, initially with the definition of the service requirements. Each stage of the development is then correlated with associated testing and validation activities according to the defined test model to be used.

14.1.4 Testing Activities:

Service Transition
- Planning and test resources
- Prioritizing and scheduling
- Management of incidents, problems, errors etc
- Consequential changes
- Capturing configuration baseline
- Test metric collection, analysis, reporting and management

Other Lifecycle activities
- Resourcing
- Hardware, networking, staff numbers and skills etc
- Business/customer resources required
- Supporting services including areas, security etc
- Schedule of milestones, delivery/handover dates etc
- Financial requirements

14.1.5 Testing Approaches:

- Document review
- Modeling and measuring
- Risk-based approach that focuses on areas of greatest risk
- Standards compliance approach
- Experience based approach
- Approach based on organizations lifecycle methods
- Simulation
- Scenario testing
- Role playing
- Prototyping
- Laboratory testing
- Regression testing
- Joint walkthrough/workshops
- Dress/service rehearsal
- Conference room pilot
- Live pilot.

14.1.6 Service Testing:

- Usability testing
- Accessibility testing
- Process and procedure testing
- Knowledge transfer and competence testing
- Performance, capacity and resilience testing
- Availability testing
- Back up testing
- Documentation testing
- Security testing
- Operability and maintainability testing etc

14.1.7 Other types of testing:

- Service requirements and structure testing
- Service level testing
- Warranty and assurance test

- o Contract and regulation testing
- o Compliance and regulation testing
- o Service Management testing
- o Operational tests
- o Regression testing

14.1.8 Design Considerations:

- o Finance
- o Documentation
- o Supplier
- o Build
- o Testable
- o Traceability
- o Where and when
- o Remediation

14.1.9 Inputs:

- o Service Package/SLP
- o Service Provider interface definitions
- o Service Design Package
- o Release & Deployment Plans
- o Acceptance Criteria
- o RFC's

14.1.10 Outputs:

- o Configuration Baseline
- o Testing carried out
- o Test results
- o Results Analysis
- o Updated data, information, knowledge to be added to SKMS
- o Test incidents, problems or error records
- o Improvement ideas for CSI
- o 3RD Party relationships, suppliers, partners, users, customers and/or other stakeholders.

14.1.11 Challenges

Most of the challenges to effective testing are based on lack of respect and understanding of its role. The result is lack of funding and therefore:
- o Inability to maintain test environments and corresponding test data
- o Insufficient staff, skills and testing tools
- o Projects over-running and allocated testing time frames reduced
- o Developing standard performance measures across projects and suppliers
- o Inaccurate estimated delivery times

14.1.12 Metrics:

- o Effort and costs to set up testing environments
- o Effort required to find defects
- o Reduction of repeat errors
- o Reduced error/defect rate in later testing stages or production
- o Re-use of testing data
- o % incidents linked to errors detected during testing
- o % of errors at each lifecycle stage
- o % of errors that could have been identified during testing
- o # known errors documented in earlier testing phases.

15 Evaluation

Objective:
- o Evaluate the intended effects of a service change and as much of the unintended effects as is reasonably practical given capacity, resources and organizational constraints.
- o Provide good quality outputs from the evaluation process so that Change Management can expedite an effective decision about whether a service change is to be approved or not.

15.1 Basic Concepts:

15.1.1 Evaluation- Business Value:

- o Effective evaluation will establish the use made of resources in terms of delivered benefit, and this information will allow a more accurate focus on value in future service development and Change Management.
- o The CSI phase can use a lot of data collected from the Evaluation process, to analyze for future improvements to the process of change and the predictions and measurements of service change performance.

15.1.2 Evaluation Plan:

- o Understanding the intended effect of a change
- o Understanding the unintended effect of a change
- o Factors for considering the effect of a service change
- o Evaluation of predicted performance
- o Evaluation of actual performance
- o Risk Management

15.1.3 Activities:

- Plan evaluation
- Evaluate Predicted performance
- Evaluate actual performance
- Risk Management
- Document Evaluation Report

15.1.4 Evaluation Report:

- Risk Profile
- Deviations Report
- Qualification Statement (if required)
- Validation Statement (if required)
- Recommendations

15.1.5 Inputs:

- Service Package
- SDP and SAC
- Test results and report

15.1.6 Outputs:

- Evaluation Report for Change Management

15.1.7 Metrics:

Customer/business KPI's are:
- Variance from service performance required by customers (minimal and reducing)
- Number of incidents against the service (low and reducing)

The internal KPI's include:
- Number of failed designs that have been transitioned (zero)

- Cycle time to perform an evaluation (low and reducing)

15.1.8 Challenges

- Developing standard performance measures and measurement methods across projects and suppliers.
- Projects and suppliers estimating delivery dates inaccurately and causing delays in scheduling evaluation activities.
- Understand the different stakeholders perspectives that underpin effective risk management
- Understand the balance between managing risk and taking risk as its affects the overall strategy.
- Encouraging a risk management culture where people share information.

16 Service Asset and Configuration Management

Objective: The objective of this process is to define and control the components of services, and infrastructure, and maintain accurate configuration information on the historical, planned and current state of the services and infrastructure.

16.1 Basic Concepts:

16.1.1 Service Asset and Configuration Management – Business Value

- Better forecasting and planning of changes
- Changes and releases to be assessed, planned and delivered successfully
- Incidents and problems to be resolved within the service level targets
- Service levels and warranties to be delivered
- Better adherence to standards, legal and regulatory obligations
- More business opportunities as able to demonstrate control of assets and services
- Changes to be traceable from requirements
- Ability to identify the costs for a service.

16.1.2 Policies

- The first step is to develop and maintain the SACM policies that set the objectives, scope, principles and CSF's for what is to be achieved by the process.
- These policies will be considered within the Change and Release & Deployment Management processes as the policies are closely related. Policies will be based on:
    - Business drivers
    - Contractual requirements
    - Service Management requirements

- Compliance to relevant regulations, laws and standards.

16.1.3 Key activities:

- Management and Planning
- Identification
- Status Accounting
- Reporting
- Verification and Audit
- Control

16.1.4 Configuration Management System

- Asset data may be made available to external financial Asset management systems for reporting.
- Maintaining relationships between all service components and any related incidents, problems, known errors etc
- Retaining corporate data about employees, suppliers, locations and business units, customers and users.
- At a data level, the CMS takes data from several physical CMDB's, which together constitute a federated CMDB. Other data sources will also plug into the CMS such as the definitive media libraries. CMS will provide access to data in asset inventories wherever possible rather than duplicating data

16.1.5 Interfaces:

- Change Management – identifying the impact of proposed changes
- Financial Management – capturing key financial information such as costs, depreciation methods, owner and user, maintenance and repair costs.
- ITSCM – awareness of assets the business services depend on, control of key spares and software

- Incident/problem/error – providing and maintaining key diagnostic information; maintenance and provision of data to the service desk
- Availability Management in detection of point of failure.

16.1.6 Metrics:

- # of discovered unauthorized configurations
- Audit reviews
- Poor impact assessment that lead to inefficient change
- Change related incidents/problems
- Cycle time to approve and implement changes
- Licenses that have been wasted or not put into use at a particular location
- Exception reports during configuration audits
- Unauthorized IT components detected in use.

16.1.7 Service Operation Activities

- Informing SACM of any discrepancies found between CI's and the CMS.
- Making amendments as necessary, under the authority of SACM, where they involve any Service Operations components or services.

16.2 Key Terms:

Configuration Item (CI): *ANY* component that supports an IT service

CMS: Configuration Management System

CMDB: Configuration Management Database

Attribute: *Specific* information about CI's.

CI Level: Recording and reporting of CI's at the level that the *business requires*.
Status Accounting: Reporting of all *current and historical* data about each CI throughout its lifecycle.

Configuration Baseline: Configuration established at a specific point in time, captures both the structure and details of a configuration. Used as a reference point for later comparison.

17 Knowledge Management

Objectives:
- Enable the service provider to be more efficient
- Ensuring staff have a clear and common understanding
- Ensuring that, at a given time and location, service provider staff have adequate information on:
  - who is currently using their services
  - the current states of consumption
  - service delivery constraints
  - difficulties faced by the customer

17.1 Basic Concepts:

17.1.1 Knowledge Management – Business Value

- Knowledge Management is especially significant within Service Transition since relevant and appropriate knowledge is one of the key service elements being transitioned.
- User, service desk, support staff and supplier understanding of the new or changed service, including knowledge of errors signed off before deployment, to facilitate their roles within that service
- Awareness of the use of the service, and the discontinuation of previous versions
- Establishment of the acceptable risk and confidence levels associated with the transition.

17.1.2 Data to Wisdom:

Data – Information – Knowledge – Wisdom

17.1.3 Development of Service Knowledge Management System (SKMS)

- SKMS – contains:
    - CMS (Configuration Management System), which contains:
        - CMDB (Configuration Management Database)

17.1.4 Knowledge Management Strategy

- Governance Model
- Organizational changes
- Establish roles and responsibilities
- Policies, processes, procedures and methods for KM
- Technology and other resource requirements
- Performance measures

17.1.5 Data and Information Management

- Establishing data and information requirements
- Define the information architecture
- Establishing data and information management procedures

17.1.6 Metrics:

- Successful implementation and early life operation of new and changed services with few knowledge-related errors
- Increased responsiveness to changing business demands
- Improved accessibility and management of standards and policies
- Knowledge dissemination
- Reduced time and effort required to support service
- Reduced time to find information for diagnosis and fixing incidents and problems
- Reduced dependency on personnel for knowledge.

18 Service Transition - Technology and Implementation

18.1 Basic Concepts:

18.1.1 Integrated ITSM technology:

- IT Service Management systems:
- Enterprise frameworks
- System, network and applications management tools
- Service dashboards and reporting tools
- Specific ITSM technology and tools that cover:
- SKMS
- Collaborative, content management, workflow tools
- Data mining tools
- Extract, load and transform data tools
- Measurement and reporting systems
- Test Management and testing tools
- Database and test data management tools
- Copying and publishing tools
- Release and deployment technology
- Deployment and logistics systems and tools.

18.1.2 Service Transition

- The task of implementing Service Transition for most service provider organizations will be one of service improvement.
- This involves assessing their current approach to the processes and establishing improvements, prioritized according to the business benefit that can be achieved.
- When setting up Service Transition attention needs to be paid to ways of quantifying and measuring the benefits, cost and in terms of what would be prevented by applying resources to any specific transition
- Useful factors to consider when designing Service Transition include:
    - Applicable standards and policies
    - Relationships

- Budget and resources

18.1.3 Service Transition –Cultural Change, Risk and Value

- Even formalization of existing procedures will deliver cultural change; if implementing Service Transition into an organization means installing formal processes that were not there before the cultural change is significant.
- The cultural change program should address all stakeholders and should continue throughout, and after, Service Transition, to ensure the changed attitudes are firmly embedded.
- As with all transitions, decisions around transitioning the transition service should not be made without adequate understanding of the expected risks and benefits.
- Risks might include:
    - Alienation of support staff
    - Excessive costs to the business
    - Unacceptable delays to business benefits.

18.1.4 Managing Communication and Commitment

- Communication –
    - Clear communication – reasons and rationale
    - Benefits expected
    - Plans for implementation and proposed effects
- Communication Strategy
- Methods of Communication
    - Large workshops
    - Organization newsletter
    - Training sessions
    - Team meetings
    - Face to face
    - Q&A feedback postings
    - Corporate internet
    - Reinforcement memos
    - Posters/roadmaps
    - Pay advice notes

18.1.5 Managing Organizational and Stakeholder Change

- Organizational roles and responsibilities
- Service Transition's role in the organizational change
- Strategy and design for managing organizational change
- Planning and implementing organizational change
- Organizational change products
- Assessing organizational readiness for change
- Monitoring progress of organizational change
- Dealing with the organization and people in sourcing changes

18.1.6 Continual Service Improvement

- Deming Cycle
    - Implementation of CSI's
    - Application of CSI to services and service management processes

18.1.7 Service Transition – Challenges

- Enabling almost every business process and service in IT
- Managing many contacts, interfaces and relationships
- Lack of integration between processes
- Inherent differences among legacy systems
- Achieving a balance – stability vs. responsiveness
- Establishing leaders to champion changes
- Establish who is doing what, when and where
- Understanding different stakeholder perspectives
- Achieving the balance between –managing risk vs. taking risk
- Evaluating effectiveness of reporting, management and governance

18.1.8 Service Transition – Critical Success Factors

- Understanding and managing the different stakeholder perspectives
- Maintaining the contacts and maintaining relationships

- Integrating with other Service Lifecycle stages
- Understanding the inherent dependencies among the legacy systems
- Automating processes to eliminate errors
- Creating and maintaining new/updated knowledge in a user-friendly form
- Developing good-quality systems, tools, processes and procedures
- Good Service Management and IT infrastructure tools and technology etc

18.1.9 Service Transition – Risks

- Change in accountabilities, responsibilities and practices
- Alienation of some key support and operations staff
- Additional unplanned costs to services in transition
- Resistance to change and circumvention of processes due to perceived bureaucracy.
- Excessive costs to the business due to overly risk adverse processes
- Knowledge sharing
- Lack of maturity and integration of systems and tools
- Poor integration between processes
- Loss of productive hours, higher costs, loss of revenue

19 Service Transition Roles

19.1.1 Roles (descriptive, not prescriptive):

- Service Transition Manager
- Change Manager
- Release and Deployment Manager
- Service Test Manager
- Service Asset and Configuration management roles
    - Configuration Manager
    - Configuration Administrator/Librarian
    - Service Asset Manager
- Knowledge Management process Owner

19.1.2 Managing Change -Service Operation Staff

- Change Triggers
- Change Assessment
- Measurement of successful change

20 Practice Exam

20.1 Refresher "Warm up Questions"

The following multiple choice questions are a refresher from the Foundation level as a prelude.

Question 1

After a Change has been implemented, an evaluation is performed. What is this evaluation called?

  a) Forward Schedule of Changes (FSC)
  b) Post Implementation Review (PIR)
  c) Service Improvement Programme (SIP)
  d) Service Level Requirement (SLR)

Question 2

What does the Service V model represent?

  a) The utility and performance requirements of new and changed services
  b) The path to Service Delivery and Service Support for efficient and effective utilization of resources
  c) A strategy for the successful completion of all IT changes
  d) Levels of Configuration and testing required to deliver a Service Capability

Question 3

Which of the following areas would technology help to support during the Service Transition phase of the lifecycle?

1. Automated workflow of ITIL processes
2. Measurement and reporting systems
3. Distribution and installation of patches
4. Performance testing of new and modified services

   a) 1, 2 and 3 only
   b) 1, 3 and 4 only
   c) 2, 3 and 4 only
   d) All of the above

Question 4

The goal of Service Asset and Configuration Management is to?

   a) Account for all the financial assets of the organization
   b) Provide a logical model of the IT infrastructure
   c) Build service models to justify ITIL implementations
   d) Provide capabilities for managing documents across the organization

Question 5

Which of the following is NOT an example of a Service Request?

   a) A user calls the Service Desk to order a toner cartridge
   b) A user calls the Service Desk because they would like to change the functionality of a standard application.
   c) A Manager submits a request for a new employee to be given access to an application
   d) A user logs onto an internal web site to download a licensed copy of software from a list of approved options

Question 6

Which of the following best describes the primary objective of Knowledge Management?

a) Auditing the configuration management system from a business perspective
b) Reducing the staffing requirements for the Service Desk and other support teams
c) To ensure reliable and secure information and data is available throughout the Service Lifecycle
d) To reduce the average Mean Time to Restore (MTTR) for incidents affecting Service availability

Question 7

Consider the following statements:
1. Service Transition provides guidance on transitioning new services into live environment
2. Service Transition provides guidance on releases
3. Service Transition provides guidance on the transfer of services to or from an external provider

Which of the above statements is CORRECT?
    a) 1 and 2 only
    b) 1 only
    c) All of the above
    d) 1 and 3 only

Question 8

Which of the following are objectives of the Release and Deployment Management process?

1. To develop a release and deployment policy
2. To ensure that training occurs for new service to operations and support staff
3. To ensure that new services are tested prior to release
4. To provide cost justifiable IT availability that is matched to the needs of the business

    a) 1, 2 and 3 only
    b) All of the above
    c) 1 and 3 only
    d) 1, 3 and 4 only

Question 9

The objective of the Change Management process is most accurately described as?

    a) Ensuring that all changes are recorded, managed, tested and implemented in a controlled manner
    b) Ensuring that emergency changes to IT infrastructure are managed efficiently and effectively
    c) Ensuring that changes have appropriate rollback plans in the event of a major incident
    d) Maximizing services by allowing changes to be made quickly

Question 10

The following options are considered within which process?

1. Big bang vs. Phased
2. Push and Pull
3. Automated vs. Manual

   a) Change Management
   b) Release and Deployment Management
   c) Service Asset and Configuration Management
   d) Knowledge Management

20.2 Intermediate Style Practice Exam

As stated at the beginning of the book, the exam is comprised of 8 scenario based multiple-choice questions (though not all exam questions contain a scenario followed by a question). The following practice exam contains 16 questions for you to complete. In the official exam, all scenarios are provided first, then the questions. To make it easier to follow due to the number of questions, we have set it out with scenario followed by question.

Scenario 1

You are a newly appointed Change Manager for a large pharmaceutical company. Until you arrival, changes were made on an adhoc level. This generated complaints from the business such as delays in simple change requests, partly completed changes, as well as lack of information sharing about upcoming changes.

The CIO has employed you to address these issues through the implementation of a Change Management Process, based on ITIL.

Question 1 (refer to Scenario 1)

What would be your initial plan to implement this process?

  a) Your first priority is to improve business satisfaction, so you analyse all incidents caused by recent changes. You then create a Request for Change form based on priority of change needs. This will then be shared with the business via a Change Schedule.

  b) It is important to ensure that all IT support staff are aware of a new change request process, so you start by communicating your vision and goals to them. You then analyse current procedures and identify improvements or good practice. To generate quick wins, you identify standard changes that can be made quickly. You establish a system for communicating changes to support staff.

51

c) It is important to ensure that all users and IT support staff are aware of a new change request process. After gaining management support, you start by communicating your vision and goals to all parties. You then analyse current procedures and identify improvements or good practice. To generate quick wins, you identify standard changes that can be made quickly. You establish a system for communicating changes to business.

d) You start by analysing all changes to identify which can be treated as standard changes, normal changes and emergency changes. You use this to generate a change model, which will be used by the organization. Following this you set up a change request procedure for all users to use.

Scenario 2

All Natural Gas (ANG) is the largest producer of natural gas products is the Asia Pacific region, providing an environmentally friendly alternative to traditional methods of electricity production. ANG has grown significantly over the last 3 years as the topic of climate change has meant that there is an increased push to develop for more sustainable practices for electricity production. Growth has also been driven by ANG's recently acquired sites in Australia with access to large quantities of natural gas.

This growth has begun to have an impact on the quality of service being offered by the IT department, while the end user population has rapidly grown over 75% in the last three years. A recent customer survey was conducted, which found that:

- Many business units have been affected by recent software releases, in some cases disrupting vital business functions for over 24 hours.
- Some customers feel that the quality of communication from the IT department has begun to drop, with little or no explanation or training being provided on how to use some of the new and modified services that have been released.
- Some business units feel restricted by the inconsistent approach towards releasing new systems and applications, as well as bug fixes and patches.
- Obtaining standard services is difficult and inconsistently managed, sometimes taking up to 3 weeks to get a standard desktop and user account deployed during busy periods.

At the same time, the IT department feels that it has been asked to manage a much larger scope of services and population of end users, without a sufficient increase in budget and staffing levels. A staff survey within the IT department was also performed, which found that:

- Many staff have been working longer hours, resulting in unpaid overtime and a more stressful working environment in general
- Staff feel that they are continually in firefighting mode, fixing issues with previously releases and dealing with incidents and

> problems as the majority of their workload
> - Staff complain that they are often unaware of what other IT groups are doing which might impact on service quality or conflict with work being performed
> - The Testing Manager has raised concern that her group is unable to perform their role due to the limited resources and time constraints placed on her by the business.
>
> With growth of ANG expected to continue, the CIO realizes the current situation is unacceptable and is investigating ways in which to improve the situation.

Question 2 (refer to Scenario 2)

Discussions have been held about the importance of the Service Transition processes and why they should be implemented within ANG. However the group responsible is having difficulty defining exactly what each of the processes will contribute. As a result some staff are arguing that Change Management should be implemented, but that Release & Deployment Management is unnecessary for ANG.

Which of the following is the BEST response describing the contributions made by Change Management and Release & Deployment Management in resolving the issues discussed in the scenario?

a)
Change Management is used to ensure that standardized methods and procedures are used for controlled, efficient and prompt handling of all IT changes. This will assist ANG by ensuring:
- Risk exposure associated with changes is optimized to reduce the potential business impact that could occur.
- Changes are always delivered successfully at the first attempt, which will assist the growth of ANG and improve customer satisfaction
- Changes are evaluated to ensure there is no undesired impact on existing IT infrastructure.

Release & Deployment Management by comparison, is focused on deploying new software releases into production, transition support to service operation staff, and ensure its appropriate performance in order to deliver value to our customers. This contributes to our goal of improving service quality by:

- Developing a consistent Release Policy which will document agreed release windows, schedules and the types of releases the IT department will deliver.
- Improving consistency in the implementation of changes across the customers, and application, hardware and project teams involved.
- Developing practices for the build, packaging, testing and distribution of software releases.

- Improve the transfer of knowledge and support to users, customers and IT support staff.

b)
Change Management is used to ensure that standardized methods and procedures are used for controlled, efficient and prompt handling of all IT changes. This will assist ANG by ensuring:
- Risk exposure associated with IT changes is optimized from both the business and IT perspectives
- Changes are delivered successfully at the first attempt, which will assist the growth of ANG and improve customer satisfaction
- Changes are evaluated appropriately so that the correct budget and resource requirements can be planned, reducing the amount of unplanned overtime currently be performed by IT staff.

Release & Deployment Management by comparison, is focused on delivering new releases into production, transition support to service operation staff, and enable its effective use in order to deliver value to our customers. This contributes to our goal of improving service quality by:

- Developing a consistent Release Policy which will document agreed release windows, schedules and the types of releases the IT department will deliver.
- Improving consistency in the implementation of changes across the IT teams, suppliers and customers involved.
- Developing repeatable practices for the build, configuration, packaging and distribution of hardware and software releases.
- Improve the transfer of knowledge and support to users, customers and IT support staff.

c)
Change Management is used to ensure that standardized methods and procedures are used for controlled, efficient and prompt handling of all changes to IT hardware and software. This will assist ANG by ensuring:
- Risk exposure associated with changes is optimized to reduce the potential impact on existing IT infrastructure.
- Changes are delivered quickly, which will assist the growth of ANG and improve customer satisfaction
- Changes are evaluated appropriately so that time is not wasted implementing changes without associated business value.

Release & Deployment Management by comparison, is focused on distributing software releases into production, transition support to service operation staff, and ensure its appropriate performance in order to deliver value to our customers. This contributes to our goal of improving service quality by:

- Developing Release and Rollout plans, which will document agreed release windows, schedules and the types of releases the IT department will deliver.
- Improving consistency in the implementation of changes across the developer and project teams involved.
- Developing repeatable practices for the building and distribution of software releases.
- Improve the transfer of knowledge and support Service Desk and second-line support staff.

d)
Change Management is used to ensure that consistent procedures are to improve the speed of all changes to IT hardware and software. This will assist ANG by ensuring:
- That IT staff record the current and historical status of IT assets and components
- Appropriate IT budgets are developed
- Capacity is appropriately planned in advance to accommodate changes.

Release & Deployment Management by comparison, is focused on distributing software releases into production, verifying the successful deployment, and reviewing any lessons learnt in order to deliver value to our customers. This contributes to our goal of improving service quality by:

- Developing Major, Minor and Emergency-Fix Releases to deliver faster change
- Improving consistency in the implementation of changes across the developer and project teams involved.
- Developing repeatable practices for the building and distribution of software releases.
- Recording all relevant knowledge in the knowledgebase.

Question 3 (refer to Scenario 2)

As part of the implementation of Release & Deployment, the documentation of an effective Release Policy is an important task. Which of the following best describes the purpose and content of a Release Policy for staff at ANG?

a)
A Release Policy is the formal documentation of the preferred strategy for releases used by ANG, and is used to govern how releases of software are implemented. Typical contents of a Release Policy include:

- How Software released will be produced
- Structure and schedules for Release Packages
- Timing of activities and events involved
- The communication plan
- Identification of new/modified CIs
- Why and where Releases should be documented
- Target CIs where releases will be deployed
- Roles and responsibilities of staff required for managing releases
- Technology to be used for releases

b)
A Release Policy is the formal documentation of the overarching strategy for releases used by ANG, and is used to govern the majority of releases being implemented. Typical contents of a Release Policy include:

- How Releases will be controlled
- Structure and schedules for Release Packages
- Definition of major and minor releases, emergency fixes
- Expected content for each type of Release
- Policy on the production and execution of back out plans
- Why and where Releases should be documented
- Blackout windows for releases based on business requirements
- Roles and responsibilities defined for the Release and Deployment process

- Technology to be used for releases

c)
A Release Policy is the formal documentation of the overarching strategy for releases used by ANG, and is used to govern the majority of releases being implemented. Typical contents of a Release Policy include:

- The level of infrastructure to be controlled by Releases
- Preferred structure and schedules for Release Packages
- Definition of major and minor releases, emergency fixes
- Expected deliverables for each type of Release
- Policy on the production and execution of back out plans
- How and where Releases should be documented
- Blackout windows for releases based on business or IT requirements
- Roles and responsibilities defined for the Release and Deployment process
- Supplier contacts and escalation points

d)
A Release Policy is the formal documentation of the overarching strategy for releases used by ANG, and is used to govern how changes are implemented. Typical contents of a Release Policy include:

- How Releases will be controlled
- Structure and schedules for Release Packages
- Definition of major and minor releases, emergency fixes
- Expected content for each type of Release
- Policy on the testing procedures
- Why and where Releases should be documented
- Blackout windows for releases based on IT requirements
- Roles and responsibilities of staff required for managing releases
- Technology to be used for releases

Scenario 3
As a newly appointed Knowledge Process Owner, you have been asked to establish a SKMS. You have engaged in discussions with relevant process owners, including Service Desk Manager, Configuration Manager and Problem Manager.

The Service Desk Manager has been with the company for 15 years and believes he has a comprehensive database that he is happy to share and build onto.

The Configuration Manager believes she too has a comprehensive CMS which could be expanded to include the Service Desk database.

From you discussions it became clear that there is a lack of knowledge and understanding about what a SKMS is and how it contributes to Knowledge Management.

Question 4 (Refer to Scenario 3)

As Knowledge Mgt Process Owner, which would be the best explanation that you would use to increase the understanding of the other 2 managers?

a) An SKMS is broken into 4 levels, based on levels of information required. It is also connected to Information security levels to ensure confidentiality of the information

b) An SKMS stores, manages, updates and presents information on all IT services and requires information from other systems and databases such as CMS and KEDB

c) An SKMS is a database that stores, manages, updates and presents information on all IT services and requires information from other systems and databases such as CMS and KEDB

d) An SKMS is part of the greater CMS which contains linkages to the KEDB and Suppliers. It should also contain information on staff experience.

Question 5 (Refer to Scenario 3)

Another area of concern is the area of the types of metrics that will be collected to understand customer benefits of such a process.

Of the following which would you identify as relevant metrics for Knowledge Management?

a) Increased responsiveness to changing IT department demands, improved accessibility and management of standards and policies, knowledge dissemination, reduced time and effort to support service

b) Increased responsiveness to changing business demands, improved accessibility and management of standards and policies, knowledge dissemination, reduced time and effort to support service

c) Increased responsiveness to changing business demands, improved accessibility and management of policies, knowledge dissemination, reduced time and effort to support service

d) Increased responsiveness to changing IT Department's demands, improved accessibility and management of CMDB, knowledge inputs, reduced time and effort to operate service

Scenario 4

3 months ago, a new critical business application was released in your Financial Planning Company. Since then users have experienced a range of similar incidents, both with this application and other applications. This has resulted in more Service Desk calls, and increased support levels.

The CIO has been under pressure by the CEO to both resolve these incidents and also to ensure that this does not occur with future application rollouts.

As Release and Deployment Manager, the CIO has asked you to review your Release Policies and procedures to analyse how these errors were not picked up during testing phase. You are required to present you analysis to the CEO and CIO along with recommendations.

You review your policies, which you find to be sound and comprehensive. You identify that testing was not completed adequately enough due to lack of knowledge and time frames.

Question 6 (Refer to Scenario 4)

Based on your analysis – which of the following would recommendations would you present to the CEO and CIO?

a) You recommend that we create a position of a dedicated Testing manager to ensure that objective levels of testing can occur. A separate testing environment will need to be set up to allow for thorough testing, so as not to affect the live environment. This would include all known errors from testing be incorporated into KEDB for future learning

b) You recommend that we create a position of a dedicated Testing manager to ensure that objective levels of testing can occur. You then recommend that this manager develop a Validation and testing process, based on ITIL Framework. A separate testing environment will need to be set up to allow for thorough testing, so as not to affect the live environment. This would include all known errors from testing and during pilot phase be incorporated into KEDB for future learning.

c) You recommend that a separate testing environment be set up to thoroughly test all applications before going live. You believe that all rollouts should occur through a pilot approach to ensure that any incidents identified in pilot can be fixed prior to full rollout.

d) You recommend that you take on role of Testing Manager as part of your Release Management responsibilities so you can identify issues in testing environment and fix them before going live. Your next step is to trial all releases in a pilot stage as part of your release strategy.

Scenario 5

As CIO of a large multi-national retail outlet, you have overall accountability for all IT services. Recently you have been receiving complaints from the business in relation to IT Project overruns in terms of cost, resources and time.

You have a mature ITIL v2 framework in place, and each process manager works closely with other process managers to ensure that a coordinated approach for transitioning services occur.

As you investigate the v3 lifecycle model you identify areas that can be improved, and hopefully address the complaints raised by the business.

One such area is the introduction of Transition, Planning and Support Process.

You raise this possibility of introducing this process and role to the other Process Managers There seems to be resistance as each manager thinks that this new role will be stepping on their toes.

Question 7 (Refer to Scenario 5)

To gain support from the other Process Managers, you highlight the scope and benefits of this process. Which of the following best represents the scope and benefits of Transition, planning and support?

a)

Scope	Benefits
o Incorporating design and operation requirements into transition plans o Managing service transition progress, changes, issues, risks and deviations o Quality review of all Service Transition, release and deployment plans o Communication with customers, users and stakeholders	o Increased ability to handle high volumes of changes and releases o Improved alignment with customer, suppliers and Project Managers

b)

Scope	Benefits
o Incorporating design and operation requirements into transition plans o Managing service transition progress, changes, issues, risks and deviations o Quality review of some release and deployment plans o Communication with users and stakeholders	o Increased ability to handle some changes and releases o Improved alignment with customer and Project Managers

c)

Scope	Benefits
o Incorporating design and operation requirements into transition plans o Managing service transition progress, changes, issues, risks and deviations o Quality review of all Service Transition, plans o Communication with customers, users and stakeholders	o Increased ability to handle high volumes of changes and releases o Improved alignment with customer, suppliers and Project Managers

d)

Scope	Benefits
o Incorporating operation requirements into support plans o Managing service operation progress, changes, issue, risks and deviations o Quality review of all Service Operations Plans o Communication with, users and stakeholders	o Increased ability to handle high volumes of RFC and Incidents o Improved alignment with customer, suppliers and Service Desk

Scenario 6

Recently, you were employed by GOGO Financial Services to streamline their rollouts of new and changed services.

You have spent this time analysing how releases are currently being managed, as well as understanding the culture of the company.

GOGO has had implemented an IT Service Management approach, but the focus is mostly on day to day support of IT. A Change Management process is in place, as is Release and Deployment, yet these are not working successfully together.

Though you have identified many issues with the current Release and Deployment process, the biggest issue is the lack of communication that occurs at all levels.

Your CIO is required to identify ways to improve the quality of IT service Management and is calling on all Process Managers to make recommendation relevant to their process.

As a relatively new process manager in the company, it is important for you to identify ways to improve service management with Release and Deployment.

Question 8 (Refer to Scenario 6)

Which of the following recommendations will you submit to your CIO?

a) You recommend that that levels of communication in relation to Release and Deployment are improved in the following ways:
   - Request minutes from CAB meetings to ensure you know what changes are occurring
   - Release schedules communicated to users
   - Set up early life support policy for new/changed services to assist Service Desk
   - Improved training on new services, focussing 1st on Service Desk, then users
   - Ensure that final acceptance occurs from customer on new service before Rollout

b) You recommend that that levels of communication in relation to Release and Deployment are improved in the following ways:
   - Greater involvement with CAB to report on release and testing issues
   - Release schedules communicated to users and IT staff
   - Set up early life support policy for new/changed services to assist Service Desk
   - Improved training on new services, focussing 1st on Service Desk, then users
   - Ensure that final acceptance occurs from customer on new service before Rollout

c) You recommend that Release and Deployment improve the way that rollouts occur by:
   - Establishing a Release Schedule
   - Defining a Release Policy
   - Defining Release Types – e.g. Big Bang, phased etc
   - Define Release Package contents
   - Establish thorough testing procedures
   - Implement Early Life Support

d) You recommend that Release and Deployment improve the way that rollouts occur by:
    - Establishing a Release Policy
    - Defining Release types – e.g. Big Bang, Phased etc
    - Train users on new service
    - Define Release Package contents
    - Establish thorough testing procedures
    - Implement Early Life Support

Question 9 (Refer to Scenario 6)

After your recommendations, your CIO is interested in knowing more about the concept of Early Life support, and why it is part of Release and Deployments' responsibility. She has asked you to list the benefits and activities for Early Life Support.

Which of the following would you present to her?

a)

Benefits	Activities
Decreased incidents Improved stability Increased customer and user satisfaction Enhanced learning Better momentum for continual improvement	Develop Early Life Support (ELS) Policy Operate service Collect service performance data Report service performance achieved Compare progress against ELS Plan Verify service stability Identify quick wins/improvements

b)

Benefits	Activities
Decreased incidents Decreased backouts Increased customer and user satisfaction Enhanced learning Better momentum for continual improvement	Operate service Develop Early Life Support (ELS) Policy Collect service performance data Report service performance achieved Compare progress against ELS Plan Verify service stability Identify quick wins/improvements

c)

Benefits	Activities
Improved stability Decreased backouts Increased customer and user satisfaction Enhanced learning Better momentum for continual improvement	Develop Early Life Support (ELS) Policy Operate service Collect service performance data Report service performance achieved Compare progress against ELS Plan Verify service stability Identify quick wins/improvements

d)

Benefits	Activities
Decreased problems Decreased backouts Increased customer and user satisfaction Better momentum for continual improvement	Operate service Develop Early Life Support (ELS) Policy Collect service feedback Report service targets achieved Compare progress against SLA Verify service stability

Question 10 (no scenario)

As Testing Manager you are responsible for designing and establishing a validation and testing process. Which of the following would be your recommended plan of attack?

a)
- Define process objectives based on business requirements and objectives
- gain management support
- Establish a testing policy
- Define resourcing requirements
- Establish roles and responsibilities with other processes and phases
- Education and awareness of Validation and testing process
- Creation of testing criteria/levels
- Set up dedicated testing environment

b)
- gain management support
- Define process objectives based on business requirements and objectives
- Define resourcing requirements
- Establish a testing policy
- Establish roles and responsibilities with other processes and phases
- Creation of testing criteria/levels
- Education and awareness of Validation and testing process
- Set up dedicated testing environment

c)
- Define process objectives based on business requirements and objectives
- Establish a testing policy
- Set up dedicated testing environment
- Establish roles and responsibilities with other processes and phases

- Define resourcing requirements
- Creation of testing criteria/levels
- Education and awareness of Validation and testing process

d)
- Define process objectives based on business requirements and objectives
- Define testing requirements
- Establish roles and responsibilities with Testing staff
- Establish a testing procedure
- Set up dedicated testing environment
- Creation of testing criteria/levels
- Education and awareness of Validation and testing process

Question 11 (no scenario)

6 months ago your large organization made a decision to use ITIL as its IT service management framework. Currently Incident problem Mgt and Service Desk have been implemented. A decision has been made to implement Change mgt next. Your design team has started to identify the correct inputs and outputs for this process. As Process design manager, you have been asked to analyze the different input and output options based on your analysis, which of the following is the correct option?

a) **INPUTS** _ Release Policy, Change Records, Operational Plans, Change Schedule, test results, evaluation report
   OUTPUTS – Approved RFCs, Rejected Change Schedules, Change to Service, New, changed CIs, Change Schedule, Change documents and records

b) **INPUTS** _ Release Policy, RFC, Change Proposal, Service Design Package, test results, evaluation plans
   OUTPUTS – Approved RFCs, Rejected RFCs, Change to Service, New, changed CIs, Change Schedule, Change documents and records

c) **INPUTS** _ Release Policy, RFC, Change Proposal, Transition Plans, Change Schedule, test results, evaluation report
   OUTPUTS – Approved RFCs, Rejected RFCs, Change to Service, New, changed CIs, Change Schedule, Change documents and records

d) **INPUTS**, RFC, Change Proposal, Transition Plans, Change Schedule, test results, evaluation plans
   OUTPUTS – Approved RFCs, Change to Service, New, changed CIs, Change Schedule, Change documents and records

Scenario 7

Your company has experienced a large growth in business offerings and annual revenue, resulting in increased staffing levels. To support the business there are 40 IT staff in the IT Service Management, including 16 on Service Desk and 9 in Service Transition.

Recently a new IT service was deployed to the business – a Customer Relationship Management (CRM) tool. This deployment was rushed through to ensure that the business could manage the increase customer volume. Negotiations between customer and Service Level Management (SLM) outlined the Service Level Requirements for this new service and was shared with the CRM tool vendor to ensure compliance. Since its deployment, SLM has received complaints that the service does not meet all the desired needs of the business. Their greatest concern was a lack of ability to integrate data from their Finance tool. This was stipulated within the associated SLA.

As Release and Deployment Manager, you were asked to "fix" the situation, as well as to ensure that future releases met business requirements.

You engage the Tool Vendor, to be told that it will incur further costs to rectify as it was not part of scope agreed to, as part of your Underpinning Contract. This was resolved, but pressure was on to improve service management so this does not occur next time. You decide to implement an Evaluation Process, based on ITIL.

Question 12 (Refer to Scenario 7)

The CIO has asked for the benefits this process will have to the business, as well as what the required role involves. Which of the following is the most appropriate?

a)

Benefit	Role
o Reduced failed designs that have been transitioned o Greater alignment between Service Provider and External Supplier requirements and actual service deployed o Identification of risks prior to deployment o Reduction in incidents from deployments	o Plan evaluation o Evaluate performance o Risk management o Liaise with Change Management o Document Evaluation Report

b)

Benefit	Role
o Reduced failed designs that have been transitioned o Greater alignment between customer and IT Department requirements and actual service deployed o Identification of risks prior to deployment o Reduction in incidents from deployments o	o Plan evaluation o Evaluate predicted performance o Evaluate actual performance o Risk management o Document Evaluation Report

c)

Benefit	Role
o Reduced failed service solutions that have been transitioned o alignment between customer requirements and service solution o Identification of risks after deployment o Reduction in incidents from deployments o	o Plan evaluation report o Evaluate performance report o Evaluate actual performance o Risk management o Document Evaluation Report

d)

Benefit	Role
o Reduced failed designs that have been transitioned o Greater alignment between customer requirements and performance o Identification of risks form performance of services o Reduction in service incidents o	o Plan evaluation report o Plan performance monitoring o Evaluate performance monitoring o Risk management o Document Performance Evaluation Report

Scenario 8

Your national company has grown considerably in the last 5 years. In the last 12 months a centralized Service Desk (CSD) was established to consolidate all resources. Prior to this, each state office had its own local service desk to provide support. Since establishing this CSD there have been numerous complaints about the effectiveness and efficiency of CSD in addressing network incidents and problems.

As IT Solutions Manager, you have been asked to review the current situation and find a solution. Through investigation you identify that the main reason for inefficiency in resolving incidents is the lack of a consolidated Configuration Management System (CMS). Though the Service desk function was centralized, each state office still maintains their own asset database.

The skill level of each secretary responsible for maintaining asset records determined format and inclusion in records.

In order to provide a more efficient and effective support service, a cohesive and integrated CMS seems to be the solution. This will help with Incident and Problem management, as well as new releases.

Question 13 (Refer to Scenario 8)

You have been asked to present to the CIO your strategy for addressing the current configuration management issues for CSD and also allow for future growth. Which of the following describes the BEST approach taken?

a) You start by creating a logical support model for CSD by identifying all applicable services that CSD needs to support. You also identify each CI associated with these services. From here you identify ways to improve the process for support management activities. Your next step is to specifically target the CSD to ensure that relevant and required information is accessible to them. You investigate possible Service Desk tools that can integrate with other areas within the IT department and also has the ability to auto detect CI's.

b) You start by creating a logical configuration model by identifying all applicable services that Configuration Management needs to support. From here you identify ways to improve the process for configuration management activities. You investigate possible CMS tools that can integrate with other areas within the IT department and also has the ability to auto detect CI's. Your next step is to specifically target the CSD to ensure that relevant and required information is accessible to them.

c) You start by creating a logical configuration model by identifying all applicable services that Configuration Management needs to support. You also identify each CI associated with these services. From here you identify ways to improve the process for configuration management activities. You investigate possible CMS tools that can integrate with other areas within the IT department and also has the ability to auto detect CI's. Your next step is to specifically target the CSD to ensure that relevant and required information is accessible to them.

d) You identify each CI associated with these services. From here you identify ways to improve the process for configuration management activities. Your next step is to specifically target the CSD to ensure that relevant and required information is accessible to them. You investigate possible CMS tools that can integrate with other areas within the IT department and also has the ability to auto detect CI's.

Scenario 9

A large organization produces and sells a range of skin care and cosmetic products. An in-house application was developed to manage all aspects of products form production to sales. Since the first major release, there have been 2 updates to this application to improved functionality based on business requirements. Both updates resulted in problems that affected the business and customer relations. These problems could have been resolved if proper testing had occurred.

A new major release of this application has been developed to allow for customers to order products online. It is vital that this release is successful.

As Transition manager, it is your responsibility to release this major upgrade. To ensure similar issues do not reoccur, you decide to set up a testing environment.
To achieve this you also decide to set up a Transition team based on ITIL guidelines to support you. This team will comprise of a Service Test manager, Release and Deployment Manager, Release Packaging and Build Manager and a Build and Test environment Manager. You also develop roles and responsibilities for each role.

However, you only have the following people available:
- Tim, who has been the application Testing Manager since the company started 6 years ago
- Claire, who has recently joined the company, but has experience in project and release management
- Michael, who is the IT Development manager.

Question 14 (Refer to Scenario 9)

As a Transition Manager, you need to assign roles to the team available. You have come up with possible options. Which option do you decide to use?

a)

Name	Roles and responsibilities
Tim	Service Test manager o design test conditions to ensure control Release Packaging and Build Manager o Manage all aspects of Release
Claire	Release and Deployment manager o build the final release
Michael	Build and test Environment manager o Ensure test environment is built to specifications

b)

Name	Roles and responsibilities
Tim	Service Test manager o design test conditions to ensure control
Claire	Release Packaging and Build Manager o build the final release
Michael	Build and test Environment manager o Ensure test environment is built to specifications Release and Deployment manager o Manage all aspects of Release

c)

Name	Roles and responsibilities

Tim	Release and Deployment manager
	   o build the final release
	Service Test manager
	   o Ensure test environment is built to specifications

Claire	Build and test Environment manager o design test conditions to ensure control
Michael	Release Packaging and Build Manager o Manage all aspects of Release

d)

Name	Roles and responsibilities

Tim	Service Test manager
	   o Ensure test environment is built to specifications
	Release and Deployment manager
	   o Manage all aspects of Release

Claire	Build and test Environment manager o build the final release
Michael	Release Packaging and Build Manager o design test conditions to ensure control

Scenario 10

A large Government organization has a very mature v2 ITIL framework in place.

An executive decision has been made to outsource the Service desk to an external provider. This provider follows best practice approach based on ITIL v3, and as such their tool includes a request Fulfilment module.

The CIO, with approval from the Executive Director has decided that this would be the perfect time to "upgrade to an ITIL v3 Framework" as they are ready to move to a more holistic service lifecycle approach to IT Service Management.

To achieve this they decided to appoint a Team Leader to manage the implementation of each phase. You are the Service Transition Manager and are responsible for overall transitioning of all new and changed services in to the Live Environment.

Question 15 (Refer to Scenario 10)

You are required to prepare a presentation to the Executive Director and CIO on how the Service Transition processes and activities are interfaced throughout the Service lifecycle. You realise that using the outsourced Service Desk as an example will help your audience to understand, and consider this when preparing your presentation.

Which of the following storylines is correct?

a)
The Service Strategy phase contributes to providing financial information as well as providing scope for these services. This will then be reflected in the Service Portfolio and updated through Change Management

At the Service Design phase, the Service acceptance criteria for the new outsourced Service Desk will be defined and agreed. The Service Design package will be created and handed over to the Service Transition Manager

Service Transition phase will ensure that the Service Desk operational criteria are tested to ensure requirements are met.

Incidents and problems learnt from testing and implementation will be shared with the outsourced Service Desk

b)
The Service Strategy phase contributes to providing financial information as well as providing scope for these services. This will then be reflected in the Service Portfolio and updated through Change Management

At the Service Design phase, the Service acceptance criteria for the new outsourced Service Desk will be tested. The Service Design package will be created and handed over to the Service Transition Manager

Service Transition phase will ensure that the Service Desk operational criteria are designed to ensure requirements are met.

Incidents and problems learnt from testing and implementation will be shared with the outsourced Service Desk

c)
The Service Strategy phase contributes to providing financial information as well as providing scope for these services. This will then be reflected in the Service Portfolio and updated through Change Management

At the Service Design phase, the Service acceptance criteria for the new outsourced Service Desk will be defined and agreed. The Service Design package will be created and handed over to the Service Transition Manager

Service Transition phase will ensure that the Service Desk operational criteria are designed to ensure requirements are met.

Incidents and problems learnt from testing and implementation will be shared with the outsourced Service Desk

d)
The Service Strategy will not be involved as outsourcing Service desk only takes place at Service Design phase

At the Service Design phase, the Service acceptance criteria for the new outsourced Service Desk will tested. The Service Design package will be created and handed over to the Service Operations Manager

Service Transition phase will ensure that the Service Desk operational criteria are designed to meet requirements. Incidents and problems learnt from testing and implementation will be shared with the outsourced Service Desk

Question 16 (No Scenario)

As Change Manager, you are required to report on the changes and issues that occur as a result of changes. These are used to assess the effectiveness and efficiency of the Change Management process.

Which of the following would you use as metrics to report on?

a)
- Number of RFCs accepted
- Number of successful changes
- Number of implemented changes
- Staff utilization
- Changed Service Utilization

b)
- Number of RFCs put through Service Desk
- Number of successful changes schedules
- Number of implemented change schedules
- Staff utilization
- Changed Service Utilization

c)
- Number of RFCs accepted
- Number of successful changes
- Number of implemented changes
- Staff utilization
- Business impact of change

d)
- Number of RFCs put through Service Desk
- Number of successful changes
- Number of implemented changes
- Staff utilization
- Changed Service Utilization

21 Answer Guide

21.1 Answers to warm up Questions

1. B
2. D
3. D
4. B
5. B
6. C
7. C
8. A
9. A
10. B

21.2 Answers to Intermediate Style Practice Exam

Remember – the way the exams are scored are on a 5/3/1/0 point scale. The following answer guide will help you to identify the most correct answer, and why it is more correct than the next answer.

Question 1

Question Rationale	This question enables the candidate to demonstrate an ability to the correct order for implementing Change Management	
Most Correct	C	Awareness and management buy in are crucial for the success of any implementation plan
Second Best	B	Same as answer C, but missing buy in
Third Best	D	These are activities once the process is implemented.
Distracter	A	You would not analyse incidents – that is Incident Management responsibility

Question 2

Question Rationale	This question enables the candidate to demonstrate an ability to differentiate between the Change, and Release & Deployment processes, communicating their different roles in an appropriate way to the scenario organization.	
Most Correct	B	Both descriptions of the contributions made by the two processes are correct. Benefits given in relation to the organization are appropriate.
Second Best	A	Change Management answer – risk only mentioning business impact, describe changes ALWAYS being delivered successfully first time, doesn't mention budget and resource requirements. Release answer – groups involved aren't correct, repeatable practices are not all mentioned.
Third Best	C	Change Management scope is incorrect (only IT hardware and software). Contributions are also not as correct as those above. Release focus and scope incorrect. Release and Rollout plans used instead of Release Policy. Other contributions only include software.
Distracter	D	Both the Change and Release answers have incorrect statements in both the scope and contributions described. In many cases they describe contributions of other ITIL processes.

Question 3

Question Rationale		This question enables the candidate to demonstrate an ability to effectively describe the correct elements and purpose of a Release Policy.
Most Correct	C	Both the purpose and typical contents are correct in the description provided.
Second Best	B	Incorrect contents: how releases will be controlled, expected content (rather than deliverables), Why and where releases should be documented, Blackout windows only based on business requirements, Technology to be used.
Third Best	D	As above, and also: policy on testing procedures, staff managing releases.
Distracter	A	As above, and also: purpose describes only software (not hardware). Remaining contents mostly come from an individual Release Plan, rather than the release policy.

Question 4

Question Rationale		This question enables the candidate to demonstrate an ability to effectively describe the correct elements of an SKMS
Most Correct	B	Correct answer according to ITIL
Second Best	C	An SKMS is more than just a database.
Third Best	D	The CMS is part of the greater SKMS – but can contain Supplier information
Distracter	A	Levels and security has nothing to do with SKMS

Question 5

Question Rationale	This question enables the candidate to demonstrate an ability to effectively describe the Metrics of Knowledge Management	
Most Correct	A	Correct answer
Second Best	B	Missing standards
Third Best	C	Focus is on IT department, not business
Distracter	D	Focus on IT department and CMDB only

Question 6

Question Rationale	This question enables the candidate to demonstrate an ability to understand the process for setting up a Testing policy	
Most Correct	B	This answer is the most logical order according to ITIL
Second Best	A	Order is correct, but a Policy needs to be created as a guiding principle for all testing
Third Best	C	There is a lot more which needs to be achieved than this
Distracter	D	You do not want the Testing manager to be same person as Release Manager.

Question 7

Question Rationale		This question enables the candidate to demonstrate an ability to demonstrate sound understanding of Transition, Planning and Support
Most Correct	A	Correct answer
Second Best	C	Missing Release Plans
Third Best	B	Benefits imply only some changes, not handle high volume, missing suppliers
Distracter	D	Focus is on Service Operation - wrong

Question 8

Question Rationale		This question enables the candidate to demonstrate an ability to understand the activities and interrelationships of Release and Deployment and other processes
Most Correct	B	Accurate activities and involvement
Second Best	A	R&D would be involved in CAB – as they have to report issues form testing so would be more than just receive minutes
Third Best	D	Question Focus is on Communication. These are more activities of R&D only – with only 1 communication example given
Distracter	C	No communication examples listed

Question 9

Question Rationale	This question enables the candidate to demonstrate an ability to demonstrate sound understanding of Early Life Support		
Most Correct	A	This is the most correct answer	
Second Best	C	Benefits are from customer perspective – decreased backouts would not be seen as a customer benefit.	
Third Best	B	Benefits are from customer perspective – decreased backouts would not be seen as a customer benefit. Also ELS policy should be developed before operation of service	
Distracter	D	Decreased problems and backouts are not customer benefits. Also order of activities incorrect	

Question 10

Question Rationale	This question enables the candidate to demonstrate an ability to correctly identify order and activities of Validation and Testing process		
Most Correct	B	This is the most correct answer	
Second Best	A	There is no point defining objectives if you do not have management support	
Third Best	C	Order is ok, but missing crucial activities	
Distracter	D	Wrong order	

Question 11

Question Rationale	This question enables the candidate to demonstrate an ability to demonstrate sound understanding of Change Management	
Most Correct	C	Correct answer
Second Best	B	Not all aspects of Service Design package would be an input to change mgt
Third Best	D	Rejected RFCs missing, and evaluation plans are not an input – but reports are
Distracter	A	Rejected change schedule does not exist, operational plans not an input

Question 12

Question Rationale	This question enables the candidate to demonstrate an understanding of the benefits and activities of Evaluation Process	
Most Correct	B	This is the most correct answer
Second Best	A	Evaluation focuses on customer needs and ensuring these are reflected – not External supplier needs
Third Best	C	Too much emphasis on just reporting – not whole process
Distracter	D	Focus is on performance (service operation) which is not objective of Evaluation

Question 13

Question Rationale		This question enables the candidate to demonstrate an ability to understand setting up a testing environment
Most Correct	B	This is the most correct answer
Second Best	D	This answer lacks the setup of the Testing process
Third Best	C	No consideration for a Testing Manager
Distracter	A	Conflict of interest. You should not be testing Manager and R&D manager

Question 14

Question Rationale		This question enables the candidate to demonstrate an ability to understand roles and responsibilities of R&D and testing, and that these should be separate responsibilities
Most Correct	B	This is the correct answer
Second Best	A	Test and Release mgr same person
Third Best	D	R&D manager – only correct responsibilities
Distracter	C	None or responsibilities against correct role

Question 15

Question Rationale		This question enables the candidate to demonstrate an ability to understand how Service Transition relies on and interfaces with other phases
Most Correct	A	This is the most correct answer
Second Best	C	Service operation criteria are not designed in Service Transition – done in Service Design, tested in transition
Third Best	B	You do not test criteria in Service Design, nor design during Transition
Distracter	D	Service Strategy is involved, in addition to reasons above.

Question 16

Question Rationale		This question enables the candidate to demonstrate CHANGE METRICS
Most Correct	C	This is the most correct answer
Second Best	A	Change Management is not concerned with changed service utilization as a metric
Third Best	D	RFCs to Service Desk is a SD metric, Change Management is not concerned with changed service utilization as a metric
Distracter	B	RFCs to Service Desk is a SD metric, Change Management is not concerned with changed service utilization as a metric. Also, focus is on change schedules – would not be uses as a metric

22 ACRONYMS

AM Availability Management
AMIS Availability Management Information System
BCM Business Capacity Management
BCP Business Continuity Plan
BIA Business Impact Analysis
CAB Change Advisory Board
ECAB Emergency Change Advisory Board
CFIA Component Failure Impact Analysis
CI Configuration Item
CMDB Configuration Management Database
CMIS Capacity Management Information System
CMS Configuration Management System
CSF Critical Success Factor
CSI Continual Service Improvement
CSIP Continual Service Improvement Program
CSP Core Service Package
DIKW Data-to-Information-to-Knowledge-to-Wisdom
DML Definitive Media Library
DS Definitive Spares
FTA Fault Tree Analysis
ISM Information Security Management
ISMS Information Security Management System
ITSCM IT Service Continuity Management
ITSM IT Service Management
IVR Interactive Voice Response
KEDB Known Error Database
KPI Key Performance Indicator
MoR Management of Risk
MTBF Mean Time Between Failures
MTBSI Mean Time Between Service Incidents
MTRS Mean Time to Restore Service
OGC Office of Government Commerce
OLA Operational Level Agreement
PBA Pattern of Business Activity
PIR Post Implementation Review
PSO Projected Service Outage

QA Quality Assurance
QMS Quality Management System
RFC Request for Change
ROI Return on Investment
SAC Service Acceptance Criteria
SACM Service Asset and Configuration Management
SCD Supplier and Contract Database
SIP Service Improvement Plan
SKMS Service Knowledge Management System
SLA Service Level Agreement
SLM Service Level Management
SLP Service Level Package
SLR Service Level Requirement
SPM Service Portfolio Management
SPOF Single Point of Failure
SSIP Supplier Service Improvement Plan
TCO Total Cost of Ownership
TQM Total Quality Management
UC Underpinning Contract
VBF Vital Business Function
VOI Value on Investment

23 Glossary

Alert: A warning that a threshold has been reached, something has changed, or a failure has occurred.

Asset: Any resource or capability.

Application Sizing: Determines the hardware or network capacity to support new or modified applications and the predicted workload.

Baselines: A benchmark used as a reference point for later comparison.

CMDB: Configuration Management Database

CMS: Configuration Management System

Configuration Item (CI): Any component that needs to be managed in order to deliver an IT Service.

DML: Definitive Media Library

Function: A team or group of people and the tools they use to carry out one or more processes or activities.

Incident: An unplanned interruption to, or reduction in the quality of an IT service

Known Error: A problem that has a documented Root Cause and a Workaround

KEDB: Known Error Database

Maintainability: A measure of how quickly and effectively a CI or IT service can be restored to normal after a failure.

Modeling: A technique used to predict the future behaviour of a system, process, CI etc

MTBF: Mean Time Between Failures (Uptime)

MTBSI: Mean Time Between Service Incidents

MTRS: Mean Time to Restore Service (Downtime)

OLA: Operational Level Agreement

Process: A structured set of activities designed to accomplish a specific objective.

Process Owner: Role responsible for ensuring that a process is fit for purpose.

Remediation: Recovery to a known state after a failed Change or Release

RFC: Request for Change

Service: A means of delivering value to Customers by facilitating Outcomes Customers want to achieve without the ownership of specific Costs and risks

Service Owner: Role that is accountable for the delivery of a specific IT service

SCD: Supplier and Contracts Database

Service Assets: Any capability or resource of a service provider

Serviceability: Measures Availability, Reliability, Maintainability of IT services/CI's under control of external suppliers.

SIP: Service Improvement Plan

SKMS: Service Knowledge Management System

SLA: Service Level Agreement

SLM: Service Level Manager

SLR: Service Level Requirements

SSIP: Supplier Service Improvement Plan

Status Accounting: Reporting of all current and historical data about each CI throughout its lifecycle.

Trigger An indication that some action or response to an event may be needed.

Tuning: Used to identify areas of the IT infrastructure that could be better utilized.

UC: Underpinning Contract

Utility: Functionality offered by a product or service to meet a particular need. Often summarized as 'what it does'.

VBF: Vital Business Function

Warranty: A promise or guarantee that a product or service will meet its agreed requirements.

24 References

ITIL. Continual Service Improvement (2007) OGC. London. TSO
ITIL. Service Design (2007) OGC. London. TSO
ITIL. Service Operation (2007) OGC. London. TSO
ITIL. Service Strategy (2007) OGC. London. TSO
ITIL. Service Transition (2007) OGC. London. TSO

Websites

www.artofservice.com.au
www.theartofservice.org
www.theartofservice.com

INDEX*

A

ability   16, 35, 76, 80-1, 90-7
   service provider☐s   16
acceptance, final   69
accessibility, improved   40, 62
accountabilities   44, 65
activities, test   23, 25, 28
actual performance   32-3, 77-8
alignment   77-8
All Natural Gas, *see* ANG
AMIS Availability Management Information System BCM   99
ANG (All Natural Gas)   53, 55-7, 59-60
ANG, growth of   54-7
answer guide   2, 90
answers   5, 7-8, 14, 90, 93, 97
APMG ITIL   1, 5
applications   7, 15, 47, 53, 55, 63-4, 82
Approved RFCs   75
Art of Service Objective Tree   2, 9
assets   12, 19, 35-6, 57
Audit   36-7
auto   80-1
Automated workflow of ITIL processes   47
Automating processes   44
availability   14, 16, 29, 49
Availability Management   37, 99

B

backouts, decreased   71-2, 95
balance   34, 43
Bang   23, 69-70
Basic Concepts   11, 16-17, 22, 27, 32, 35, 39, 41
Benefit Role   77-8
benefits   3, 9, 20, 41-2, 66, 71, 77, 91, 94-6
Benefits Activities Decreased   71
Better momentum   71-2
Blackout windows, documented ☐   59-60
book   1, 3, 51
Build
   Claire   84
   Michael   83
Build Manager   83-4
business   7, 11, 17-18, 22, 25, 27, 38, 42, 44, 49, 51-2, 54, 56, 60, 65, 76-7 [2]

business benefits   41-2
Business Capacity Management   99
Business/customer resources   28
business demands, changing   40, 62
Business Function   53, 103
business impact   89, 91
business process   43
business requirements   73-4, 76, 82, 92
   customer□s   27
business requirements □ Roles   59
business services   36
business units   36, 53
Business Value   27, 35, 39

C

CAB   20-1, 69, 94
candidate   90-8
capabilities   12, 47, 101-2
   specialized organizational   12
capacity   14, 16, 29, 32
case study/scenario   7
centralized Service Desk, see CSD
CEO   63-4
Challenges   20, 25, 31, 34, 43
Change and Release answers   91
change documents   19, 75
Change Management   2, 15-17, 19, 21, 32, 36, 50, 55-7, 86-7, 91, 96, 98
   implementing   90
   stakeholder   17
Change Management activities   18
Change Management and Release   55
Change Management answer   91
Change Management Policies   17, 27
Change Management process   18, 49, 68, 89
Change Management Process   51
Change Management support tools   18
Change Model Process   18
Change Proposal   19, 75
change request process   51-2
Change schedule   19-20, 98
Change Schedule   21, 51, 75
changed CIs   75
changed service utilization   89, 98
changed services   15, 22, 27-8, 39-40, 46, 68, 85
CI (Configuration Item)   19, 21, 38, 80-1, 101-3

CIO   51, 54, 63-5, 68-9, 71, 77, 80, 85
CI☐s   19, 37-8, 80-1
Claire Release   83
CMDB   26, 38, 40, 62, 93, 101
CMIS Capacity Management Information System CMS   99
CMS (Configuration Management System)   36-8, 40, 48, 61, 79, 92, 99, 101
CMS tools   80-1
Commitment   20
communication   15, 18, 42, 53, 66-9, 94
company   3, 61, 68, 76, 82
comparison   38, 55-8, 101
complaints   65, 76, 79
components   24, 26, 37-8, 57, 101
concept   1, 7, 10, 71
configuration   38, 46, 56
configuration audits   23, 25, 37
configuration baseline   28, 30, 38
Configuration Item, *see* CI
Configuration Management   20, 23, 80
configuration management activities   80-1
Configuration Management Database   38, 40, 101
configuration management roles   45
Configuration Management System, *see* CMS
contacts   43
contents, expected   59-60, 92
continual improvement   19, 71-2
contributions   55, 91
control   12, 35-6, 103
control Claire Release Packaging   83
control Michael Release Packaging   84
control Release Packaging   83
controlled ☐ Structure   59-60
Correct answer   92-4, 96-7
costs   11-12, 31, 35-6, 41, 44, 49, 65, 76, 102
Creation of testing criteria/levels   73-4
CRM (Customer Relationship Management)   76
CSD (centralized Service Desk)   79-81
cultural change   42
culture   17, 20, 68
customer base   16
customer benefits   62, 95
Customer/business KPI   33
customer centric   7
customer perspective   95
customer relations   82

Customer Relationship Management (CRM)   76
customer satisfaction ☐ Changes   57
customer survey   53
customer volume   76
customers   11-12, 14-15, 20-2, 25, 27-8, 30, 33, 36, 39, 53, 55-8, 66-7, 69, 76-7, 82, 96 [1]

D
databases   13, 41, 61, 92
Decreased customer dissatisfaction   25
Define Release Package contents   69-70
Defining Release types   70
Defining Release Types   69
Definitive Media Library (DML)   26, 101
demonstrate   4, 90-7
demonstrate sound understanding   94-6
department   53, 55-7, 77, 80-1, 93
deployment   2, 15, 19, 22-3, 25, 39, 41, 58, 68-70, 76-8, 94
Deployment Management   50
Deployment Management process   49
deployment manager   45, 63, 76, 82-4
deployment models   23-4
deployment plans   22, 24, 66
deployment process   60, 68
deployment process copyright   59
design test conditions   83-4
designations   3
developer   57-8
Development of Service Knowledge Management System   40
deviations   66-7
Distracter   90-8
DML (Definitive Media Library)   26, 101
document   21, 55-7
Document Evaluation   77-8
documentation
    changed Service Management   24
    formal   59-60

E
Early Life Support (ELS)   26, 71-2, 95
early life support policy   69
Education   73-4
effort   31, 40, 62
elements, correct   92
ELS, see Early Life Support
ELS Plan   71-2

emergency   20, 59-60
emergency changes   49, 52
Emergency-Fix Releases   58
Enhanced learning   71-2
entry criteria   23-4
environment, live   26, 48, 64, 85
errors   28, 31, 39, 44, 63
Establishing data   40
evaluation   2, 16, 19, 32, 34, 46, 96
Evaluation- Business Value   32
Evaluation Plan   32, 75, 96
Evaluation Report for Change Management   33
exam   1, 7, 51, 90
Excessive costs   42, 44
execution   59-60
exit   23-4
Expert status   4

F
failure   37, 99-102
fit   16, 27, 102
focus   11, 32, 68, 93-4, 96, 98
Forward Schedule of Changes (FSC)   46
FSC (Forward Schedule of Changes)   46
functions   12, 101

G
groups   12, 54-5, 91, 101
growth   53, 80
guidance   48

H
handling, prompt   55-7
hardware   12, 26, 28, 55-7, 91-2, 101

I
Identification of risks   77-8
implementation   2, 19, 41-2, 51, 55-9, 85-8
Improved alignment   66-7
Incident and Problem management   79
incident management   26, 28, 90
Incident problem Mgt and Service Desk   75
incidents   20, 25-6, 28, 31, 33, 35-6, 48-9, 51, 53, 63-4, 67, 77-8, 86-8, 90, 101
Incorporating design   66-7
Increased ability   66-7

Increased customer   25, 71-2
Increased responsiveness   40, 62
information   3, 5, 25-6, 30, 32, 34, 38-40, 48, 51, 61
  financial   36, 86-7
  required   80-1
  supplier   92
infrastructure   12, 26, 35, 47, 49, 55, 57, 60, 103
input   18, 75, 96
Inputs   19, 24, 30, 33
INPUTS   75
integration   17, 43-4
interfaces   18, 20, 36, 43, 97
Intermediate Service Transition   1, 5
ISMS Information Security Management System ITSCM   99
ITIL   1-2, 4, 6-7, 9, 14, 51, 75-6, 85, 92-3, 104
ITIL implementations   47
ITIL Intermediate Service Transition Exam   6
ITIL Intermediate Service Transition Syllabus   1
ITIL processes   11, 91
ITIL Service Lifecycle   10
ITSM   7, 9, 11-12, 99

K
KEDB   61, 64, 99, 101
Key Terms   12, 21, 26, 38
knowledge   1, 7, 30, 39-40, 44, 58, 61, 63
  transfer of   15, 29, 56-7
knowledge dissemination   40, 62
Knowledge Management   2, 15-16, 39, 48, 50, 61-2, 93
Knowledge Management process Owner   45
Knowledge Mgt Process Owner   61
Known Error   31, 36, 64, 101

L
levels   9, 26, 28, 38, 60-1, 68, 92
levels of availability   14, 16
levels of communication   69
liability   3
lifecycle   4, 7, 14, 38, 47, 103
locations   36-7, 39
London   1, 104
Low customer satisfaction   11

M
maintainability   29, 102-3
maintenance   36-7

management   11, 18-20, 28, 36, 43, 62, 77, 90, 98
management support   52, 73, 95
manager   11, 47, 61, 64-5, 97
  process design   75
  test Environment   83-4
manages   61
Managing service transition   66-7
Mean Time to Restore (MTTR)   17, 48, 99, 102
Mean Time to Restore Service   99, 102
metrics   20, 25, 31, 33, 37, 40, 62, 89, 98
Metrics of Knowledge Management   93
Michael Release Packaging   84
Missing Release Plans   94
models   18, 24, 28, 46
  logical configuration   80
Most Correct   90, 92-8
most correct answer   5, 90, 95-8
MTTR (Mean Time to Restore)   17, 48, 99, 102

N
Name Roles   83-4
New tested service capability   24
Number   33, 89

O
objective levels   64
OGC   104
operation requirements   66-7
operational criteria   86-8
organization   9, 11-12, 14, 18, 22, 27, 42-3, 47, 52, 91
Organizational changes   40, 43
Organizational roles   43
organizations release policy   26
outcomes customers   12, 102
outputs   19, 22, 24, 30, 33, 75
  evaluation report   75
overarching strategy   59-60
ownership   12, 100, 102

P
packaging   55-6
performance measures, standard   25, 31, 34
person   3, 12, 93, 97
phases   8, 11, 31, 63, 73, 85, 97
PIR (Post Implementation Review)   21, 46
Plan evaluation   33, 77

Plan evaluation report   78
plans □   59-60
policies   19, 27, 35, 40-1, 62-3, 71-2, 92-3
   testing   73, 93
Post Implementation Review (PIR)   21, 46
Practice Exam   1-2, 46, 51
presentation   86
priority   51
problems   28, 30, 35-6, 40, 54, 79, 82, 101
problems learnt   86-8
Process Managers   11, 65-6, 68
process objectives   73-4
Process Owner   61, 102
   appointed Knowledge   61
processes
   evaluation   32, 76, 96
   formal   42
   re-useable   25
production   15, 25, 31, 55-60
   electricity   53
products   3, 11, 103
progress   66-7, 71-2
Project Managers   66-7
project teams   55, 57-8
projects   17, 25, 31, 34, 82
publisher   3

Q
quality review   66-7

R
Rationale   90-8
R&D   94, 97
recommendations   33, 63-4, 68-9, 71
Reduction   20, 31, 77-8
refresher   46
Regression   29-30
regulations   30, 36
Rejected RFCs   75, 96
Release & Deployment   59
Release & Deployment Management   16, 55-8
Release & Deployment Management processes   35
Release & Deployment Plans   30
Release & Deployment processes   91
Release and Deployment   2, 22, 68-70, 94
Release and Deployment Management   50

Release and Deployment Management process   49
Release and Deployment manager   83-4
Release and Deployment Manager   45, 63, 76, 82
Release and Deployment Models   23
Release and Deployment plans   22
Release and Deployment process   60
Release and Deployment process Copyright   59
Release and Deployments☐ responsibility   71
Release and Rollout plans   91
Release Copyright   83
release design   24
release management   26, 64, 82
Release Manager   93
release mgr   97
Release Packages   22, 26, 59-60
Release Packages ☐ Timing   59
Release Packaging and Build Manager   82
Release Policy   24, 27, 59-60, 63, 69-70, 75, 91-2
  consistent   55-6
  effective   59
release promotion   23
Release Schedule   69
release scheduling   18
release strategy   64
Release Unit   26
release windows   55-7
release ☐ policy   59-60
releases   15-16, 19, 22-6, 28, 35, 41, 48-9, 53, 55-7, 59-60, 64, 66-9, 76, 79, 82-4, 92 [1]
  comprehensive   22
  final   83-4
  managing   92
  minor   59-60
  ☐ Developing   57
releases Copyright   60
releases ☐   60
requirements ☐ Roles   60
resources   12, 15, 19, 23, 32, 42, 46, 65, 79, 101-2
resourcing requirements   73-4
responsibilities   17-18, 23, 40, 43-4, 59-60, 73-4, 82-4, 97
responsibilities of staff   59-60
RFCs   19, 21, 67, 75, 89, 102
RFCs to Service Desk   98
RFC☐s   19-20, 30
risk management   33, 77-8
risks   12, 17, 19, 25, 27, 34, 39, 42-4, 66-7, 77-8, 91, 99, 102

managing   34, 43
roles   8, 11, 18, 23, 31, 39-40, 45, 54, 64-5, 73-4, 82-3, 91, 97, 102
rollouts   64, 68-70

S
scenario   5, 7-8, 29, 51, 53, 55, 59, 61-6, 68-9, 71, 73, 75-7, 79-80, 82-3, 85-6, 89
scenario organization   91
schedules   55-7, 59-60
scope   22, 35, 53, 66, 76, 86-7, 91
Scope Benefits   66-7
SD metric   98
Second Best   90, 92-8
security   16, 28-9, 92
Service   12, 26-8, 46, 66-7, 75, 101-2
Service & Business Continuity Plans   24
service acceptance criteria   86-8
Service Asset and Configuration Management   2, 15, 35, 47, 50
Service Asset and Configuration management roles   45
service availability   48
Service Capability Copyright   46
service change   32
service Change Management process   17
service components   26, 35-6
Service Design   86-8, 96-7, 104
Service Desk   37, 39, 47-8, 61, 63, 67, 69, 75-6, 85-9
   new outsourced   86-8
   outsourced   86-8
Service Desk Manager   61
Service Improvement Programme (SIP)   46, 103
service incidents   78, 99, 102
Service Knowledge Management System, *see* SKMS
Service level   16, 21, 29, 35
Service Level Agreement   100, 103
Service Level Management (SLM)   76, 103
Service Level Requirement (SLR)   46, 76, 100, 103
Service Lifecycle   2, 9, 14, 16, 48, 86
Service Management   2, 4, 9-11, 15, 22, 30, 68, 76, 85, 99
service management processes   16-17, 43
Service Operations   37, 94, 96, 104
Service Package   24, 33
service performance, service performance data Report   71-2
Service Portfolio   86-7
Service Providers   14, 25, 30, 39
service quality   53-4
   improving   55-8

service requirements   22, 28-9
service stability   71-2
service stability Copyright   72
Service Strategy   86-7, 97, 104
Service Test   82, 84
Service Transition   1-2, 8, 15-16, 22, 25, 28, 39, 41-4, 47-8, 76, 86-8, 97, 104
  implementing   41-2
Service Transition Manager   45, 85-7
Service Transition Phase   10, 28
Service Transition practices   15, 22
Service Transition processes   55, 86
Service Transition Processes   15
Service Transition Program, accredited ITIL   10
Service Transition Roles   2, 45
Service Validation   2, 15, 27
Serviceability   103
services   3, 11-16, 19-20, 25-8, 33, 35, 37-9, 41, 43-4, 48, 61, 71-2, 76-8, 80-1, 86-7, 101-3 [3]
  applicable   80
  new   48-9, 69-70, 76
  new/changed   69
set   12, 31, 35, 51-2, 64, 69, 73-4, 82
SIP (Service Improvement Programme)   46, 103
situation   54, 76, 79
skills   28, 31
SKMS (Service Knowledge Management System)   30, 40-1, 61, 92, 103
SKMS Service Knowledge Management System SLA   100
SLM (Service Level Management)   76, 103
SLP   24
SLR, *see* Service Level Requirement
software   12, 26, 47, 57, 59, 91-2
software releases   53, 55-6, 59
  distributing   57-8
  distribution of   55, 57-8
specifications   24, 28, 83-4
staff   39, 53, 55-6, 59-60, 69, 76, 92
  service operation   45, 55-7
staff utilization   89
stakeholders   12, 14, 18, 22, 30, 42-3, 66-7
standardized methods   55-7
standards   25, 35-6
  management of   40, 62
start   8, 51-2, 80
state office   79
Status Accounting   36, 38, 103

steps, next 64, 80-1
suppliers 20, 22, 25, 30-1, 34, 36, 56, 61, 66-7
support service 40, 62
support staff 39, 42, 49, 51-2, 56
systems 13, 22-3, 26, 41, 44, 47, 51-3, 61, 102
   legacy 43-4
   service management 41

T

Table of Contents 2
team 12, 56, 82-3, 101
technology 2, 11, 22, 24, 40-1, 44, 92
Template release 23
terminology 10
Test and Release mgr 97
test environments 23, 31, 83-4
test results 19, 30, 33, 75
testing criteria/levels 73-4
testing environment 31, 64, 82, 97
   dedicated 73-4
Testing Manager 54, 64, 73, 93, 97
   dedicated 64
Third Best 93-8
Tim Release 84
Tim Service Test 83-4
timescales 17-18
tools 9, 12, 18, 23, 31, 41, 44, 76, 85, 101
traceability 22, 30
trademarks 3
transition 15, 19, 39, 41-2, 44, 65-7, 94, 97
transition manager 82-3
transition plans 66-7, 75
transition support 55-7
tree 9
TSO 104
Typical contents 59-60, 92

U

unauthorized changes 17-18, 20
unintended effects 32
updates 61, 82
user satisfaction 25, 71-2
users 13, 15, 22, 30, 36, 39, 52-3, 56, 63, 66-7, 69
Utility 16, 103

V

validation 27-8, 64, 73, 95
  awareness of 73-4
value 1, 11-12, 16-17, 22, 27, 32, 42, 55-8, 102
  associated business 57
Value of Service Transition 16
vision 51-2

W
Warranty 16, 29, 103
ways 7, 22, 41, 54, 68-70, 80-1, 90-1
web 5, 7
wins/improvements 71-2

LaVergne, TN USA
10 September 2009
157471LV00003B/249/P